LET'S VISIT VIETNAM

Let's visit VIETNAM

BERNARD NEWMAN

ACKNOWLEDGEMENTS

The Publishers are grateful to the Author and to the following individuals and organisations for permission to reproduce the photographs included in this book:

Barnaby's Picture Library; Camera Press Ltd.; the Embassy of Vietnam; Photomedia; Skyport Fotos and the United States Information Service.

The cover photograph of a rice-planter at work is reproduced by permission of Camera Press Ltd. and was taken by William Warbey.
The Publishers are also grateful to Garry Lyle for assistance in preparing this new edition.

CIP data
Newman, Bernard
   Let's visit Vietnam. – 3rd ed.
   1.   Vietnam – Social life and customs – Juvenile literature
   I.   Title
   959.7   DS557.A5
   ISBN 0 222 00922 5

Burke Publishing Company Limited
Pegasus House, 116-120 Golden Lane, London EC1Y 0TL, England.
Burke Publishing (Canada) Limited
Toronto, Ontario, Canada.
Burke Publishing Company Inc.
540 Barnum Avenue, Bridgeport, Connecticut 06608, U.S.A.
Filmset in 'Monophoto' Baskerville by Green Gates Studios, Hull, England.
Printed in Singapore by Tien Wah Press (Pte) Ltd.

Contents

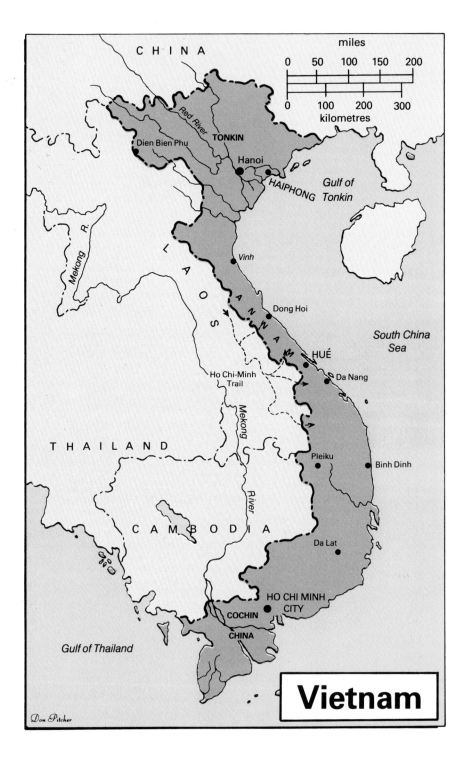

The Early Days

About three thousand years ago there lived in the country now called Vietnam a prince named Lai-Long-Quan. He, it is said, married a fairy named Au-Co. Instead of having babies, she laid a hundred eggs!

They all hatched out sons and, as the boys grew up, fifty of them went north with their mother, and founded China. The others, with their father, settled south of China in the Red River delta, and founded Vietnam.

This is, of course, only a legend—though there are still plenty of people who believe it!

In fact, Malay tribes from the islands now called Indonesia came to Vietnam early in its history. Indians also settled there —and both peoples have had their effects on the Vietnamese way of life and on the language.

The Indonesians belonged to a nation named the Chams; they were distinct from the other Malay peoples, and formed their own kingdom called Champa.

In 111 B.C. the northern part of what is now Vietnam was conquered by the armies of the Chinese emperor. Later, Chinese rule extended south and lasted nearly a thousand years. Champa and the other small kingdoms were conquered—though a few thousand Chams still survive in Vietnam. The power of China was supreme.

This fact has been important in our own times. When China became a communist country in 1949, its new rulers proclaimed their intention of restoring the boundaries of ancient China. Any region which was once ruled by China—or which paid tribute to the Chinese emperor—ought, they said, to belong to China again. Hence there is much Chinese interest in modern Vietnam.

Two thousand years ago Chinese power was strongest in the northern section of Vietnam. This consisted of two provinces, called Tonkin and Annam.

Annam means "the pacified south", yet Annam was far from being pacified. Its Vietnamese people often revolted against the Chinese yoke. In A.D. 40 one of the Vietnamese noblemen was executed. His widow and her sister, Trung-Toc and Trung-Nhi, raised an army, slaughtered the Chinese garrison and became joint queens. Though they were later defeated, the Trung sisters are often described as the Vietnamese Joans of Arc. Joan was declared to be a saint, but the Trung sisters are actually worshipped as gods.

Not until A.D. 939 were the Chinese expelled from Vietnam. Then the people of Annam began to quarrel among themselves, for their feudal lords could never agree. However, they still managed to defeat and overrun the independent kingdom

One of the small minority of Chams who live in Vietnam today. Their ancestors came to Vietnam from Indonesia many years ago

A Vietnamese farmer working in the rich rice-fields of the south

of Champa to the south of Annam, and to take the delta lands of the Mekong River from a neighbouring kingdom.

Now their country consisted of the fertile deltas of the Red River and the Mekong (which you can see on the map), connected by a narrow strip of mountainous country. Today the Vietnamese often call their country a *don ganh*—a carrying pole—which, when carried over the shoulder, supports a rice basket at each end. The two deltas are like its rice baskets.

The local lords were fierce rivals, and Vietnam was divided by conflicts rather like a civil war. When the Mekong faction won, Vietnam became a unified country under one emperor. But it still consisted of three provinces—from north to south: Tonkin, Annam and Cochin China.

Its population grew to more than thirty million—by far the greater part living in the two "rice baskets".

10

French Rule

Some of the emperors were enlightened rulers. One of them, nearly a thousand years ago, held elections for a parliament and chose his civil servants by competitive examination! Generally, however, there was no pretence at democracy. Ignorant and incompetent emperors were shut off from the rest of the world until Christian missionaries from France began to take an interest in Vietnam and its neighbours.

For many years, the missionaries were welcomed, but in 1858 some of them were murdered by Vietnamese, and this gave France an excuse to move soldiers in. The soldiers had guns—and the Vietnamese were still fighting with bows and arrows. At one time the emperor appealed to China for aid, but the French beat both countries with ease.

Soon they were masters, not only of Vietnam, but of its neighbours Laos and Cambodia. Gradually, the French imposed a system of law and order such as Vietnam had never before enjoyed. They made roads and railways, built hospitals and schools, and improved the standard of living.

True, the first French efforts at education were slow but this was largely because of language difficulties. As soon as large numbers of local young people had been trained as teachers, great progress was made. By 1944, about half the total population of school age children attended school—but the proportion was much higher in the towns and much lower in the mountain districts. There were plenty of local teachers—

the teaching staff consisted of 660 French teachers and 19,163 Vietnamese teachers.

The French began to allow local people into the civil service—but there were still many more French officials than Vietnamese ones. Later, the French tried to put this right, but there was much discontent in the land.

Vietnamese feeling was also affected by the progress of Japan—which, in a couple of generations, had advanced to become a great industrial and world power. "Asia for the Asiatics!" the Vietnamese began to say, then to shout.

By the end of the First World War, in 1918, there was a real attempt to gain independence for Vietnam. The more education the French gave to the local people, the more they

As well as training Vietnamese teachers, the French built many schools. This one had its name written in French over the entrance

wanted to rule themselves. They said, for example, that France was "exploiting" Vietnam and growing rich on Vietnamese products.

In the late 1930s the French made some concessions to the rising demands for independence: but they were too few, too little and too late.

The Japanese occupied Vietnam during the Second World War. When they were beaten, in 1946, Vietnam, Laos and Cambodia again came under French rule.

In 1890 a boy was born in Annam and named Nguyen Ai Choc. In fact, there are only about a dozen family names in Vietnam, and one person in three belongs to the Nguyen clan. (The family name is used first in Vietnam.)

But it is common for a Vietnamese to choose his own name when he grows up. When he became a man, this Annamese boy was not very modest: he chose the name Ho Chi Minh— He Who Shines.

He had been educated by the French, and then worked as a cook on board ship—and as a pastry-cook in a London hotel. In later life he still liked to prepare meals for his guests. He joined the French Communist party, and was later trained in the U.S.S.R. in sabotage and guerrilla warfare. Then he went to China where he fought for the communists.

So, by the time the Second World War ended, he was an experienced communist agent. He had a small but well-armed force. The French under-estimated him and the influence he commanded. At first, he bargained with them for Vietnamese independence. The French granted local home rule—but this did not satisfy Ho Chi Minh. He wanted Vietnam to be completely free of the French, and under a communist government.

His forces, mostly guerrillas, were called the Vietminh. They began to attack outlying French units. The French tried to fight the Vietminh by European methods, and failed. The Vietminh were lightly armed and could move quickly and easily; often their members were soldiers by night and peasant farmers by day.

The war dragged on for years. The French won minor successes, but could never bring the Vietminh guerrillas to battle. At last, the French established what they called a "hedgehog" in Vietminh territory—a fort entirely supplied from the air. With Chinese weapons, the Vietminh attacked and captured this fort, named Dien Bien Phu, and the war was over.

A conference at Geneva in 1954 made what it hoped would be a final agreement on Vietnam. The northern half of the country was handed over to Ho Chi Minh and his friends— that is, to communist rule. The southern half—with the capital, Saigon—remained independent. It was hoped that it would become a democratic state.

This hope soon faded. But, before we describe what then happened to Vietnam, let us look at the country itself and its people.

The Land and How It Is Divided

The area of Vietnam is about 128,000 square miles (330,000 square kilometres). The division in 1954 created two almost equal parts, with almost equal numbers of people. Then, the population was about 32,000,000. It has since risen sharply to about 55,000,000.

The map on page 6 shows the location of Vietnam. The general area, including Vietnam and neighbouring Cambodia and Laos, is often called Indochina, or the Indochina Peninsula. The map shows us that this area is bounded by the South China Sea on the east and the Gulf of Thailand on the west (both parts of the Pacific Ocean). To the north, it is bounded by Vietnam's third neighbour, China.

The weather is always hot in Vietnam. The average temperature is 85°F (29·5°C.) It is also very humid. This

A familiar scene in Vietnam during the monsoons: a flooded street

means that, even during the dry season, the air is always filled with moisture. The rainy season, called the monsoon, lasts from late May to the end of September. During this period many parts of Vietnam become flooded.

One of the world's longest rivers, the Mekong, flows through the south-western part of Vietnam. This river begins to the east of Tibet and flows through parts of China, Thailand, Laos and Cambodia before entering Vietnam and emptying into the South China Sea. The land around the delta of the Mekong River is flat and wet. There are swamps and vast areas of rice-fields.

The Mekong River delta is flat, and there are other flat areas along the coast and in the valley of the Song Ka, or Red River. This is Vietnam's second largest river, and it flows across the northern end of the country. On it, about 100 miles (161 kilometres) from the sea, is the city of Hanoi, now Vietnam's capital.

Apart from the flat areas already mentioned, Vietnam is hilly or mountainous. There are many mountain ranges 5,000 feet (1,525 metres) high and several as high as 8,000 feet (2,440 metres). The mountains, and some of the flat areas too, are covered with very thick jungles. Since there is heavy rainfall in Vietnam, trees, bushes and grass grow fast. The jungle trees are often very tall and so close together that sunlight cannot reach the jungle floor. Some of the hills are covered with bushes, vines and a tall grass called elephant grass.

Vietnam's largest cities are located near the sea, on the flat coastal plains. Ho Chi Minh City (formerly Saigon) is north of the big Mekong River delta. With the population of over 3,500,000, it is by far the largest city. Ho Chi Minh City is really two cities. One part is called Cholon and is almost entirely inhabited by Chinese. Some maps show Ho Chi Minh City and Cholon as separate cities, but the one runs into the other. Ho Chi Minh City is located on a navigable river and big ships sail up to it from the South China Sea.

Vietnam's second largest city is the capital Hanoi. Hanoi's population is about 2,500,000. Although on the Red River, Hanoi does not have much shipping, as the river at that point

The town hall in Saigon (now Ho Chi Minh City)

A scene in one of Vietnam's busy ports

is too shallow for large vessels. Vietnam's main port is Haiphong, in the delta—about 55 miles (88 kilometres) down river from Hanoi. Haiphong is Vietnam's third largest city, with a population of nearly 1,300,000.

The People of Vietnam and Their Language

The Vietnamese are not all of the same race. In the big rice deltas they are of Chinese stock. *Viet* means "people", and *Nam* is a Chinese word meaning "south". So Vietnam means "people of the south", or "people south of China".

About seventy-five per cent of Vietnam's people are the true Vietnamese, a people who belong to the Mongolian or yellow branch of the human family. These Chinese-like people moved from Central China to the South China coast and finally into Vietnam several thousands of years ago. They settled in the fertile river valley and along the coastal plains. They pushed the primitive tribespeople back into the mountains. The darker-skinned Chams were often attacked, some also were pushed inland and, in time, many of the people intermarried.

Most of Vietnam was once a part of China, and its people have been more influenced by China than by any other country. The Vietnamese language is somewhat like Chinese, but has also been influenced by the Khmer language of Cambodia. There are three different dialects, spoken in the north, in the central part and in the south. The language, like Chinese, is *tonal*. This means that each word can have several meanings, depending on the tone in which it is pronounced. The dialect spoken around Hanoi in northern Vietnam has six different tones; the southern dialect has five tones.

The people of Thailand and Cambodia have had written languages for centuries. These developed through contacts with India and are based on the ancient Sanskrit, the written language of India. It is strange that, until the European missionaries came to Vietnam, there was no written language there. Scholarly people, particularly in the north, often knew and used the Chinese language. Many educated people used Chinese until 1900. But most people had no way to write at all until Portuguese and French missionaries developed a written language called *Quoc-ngu*. This language, using the letters of the Roman alphabet, is still used and is the only written language for most people.

Quoc-ngu is a phonetic language. This means that the letters of the alphabet are used to spell out words as they sound. In the Vietnamese alphabet there are six simple vowels. These are *a, e, i, o, u* and *y*. By using little marks over

This photograph of a ceremony to commemorate the Trung Sisters shows Chinese and Quoc-ngu inscriptions

or under the letters, six more vowel sounds are made. These marks are called diacritical marks. Here is one example of how a simple vowel, *a*, is changed into another vowel. By writing it like this *ă*, the vowel with a short *a* sound is formed.

The *d* is pronounced as *z* in North Vietnam and as *y* in South Vietnam. The *x* is given an *s* sound in all parts of Vietnam.

We can begin to understand that Western visitors to Vietnam must have a hard time learning the language when we find that there are other marks used over or above letters to show which *tone* should be used in pronouncing a word. Let's take a simple word *ma*, which in the North Vietnam language has six tones and even more than six different meanings!

ma — with a level pronunciation or tone means   *ghost*

má — with a high tone and mark over the *a* means   *mother* or *cheek*

mà — pronounced in a low tone and with a different mark over the *a* means   *but, that* or *which*

mã — with a wavy or rising tone and a wavy mark over the *a* means   *clever* or *tomb*

ma — pronounced with a sort of break like *Ma-a* means   *house*

mạ — with a heavy tone and with a mark under the *a* means   *rice seedling*

Think of all the silly mistakes one can make by using the wrong tone! You might want to ask, "Where is your mother?"

22

If the wrong tone is used, you might ask, "Where is your tomb?" Or, "Where is your rice seedling?"

Though the Vietnamese were originally of Chinese stock, through the centuries they have intermarried with other settlers—especially with Indians and Indonesians. They live in the two great deltas and in a narrow strip of coastal plain connecting these. In the deltas the population is dense.

Of the fifty-five million total population, about fifty million live on the plains, occupying less than one-fifth of the national territory. The rest are spread very sparsely over mountainous areas. These people form the minority populations, quite distinct from the real Vietnamese.

In the south-west, near the frontier, there are many groups of Khmers, or Cambodians. Further north are tribes of Thai stock—distant cousins of the Siamese of Thailand. Even more distant relatives are the darker-skinned Laotians, who also live near the frontier. There is a resemblance between the Thai and Laotian languages, though these have been separated for hundreds of years.

Then in the mountain regions there are tribes of Moï. The name means "savages", for it was only about a hundred years ago that their neighbours admitted that the Moï were human beings and had souls. Needless to say, the Moï were and are human beings, and they do not deserve the name "savages". Indeed, it is no longer used, and the people are now called mountain peasants, or Montagnards.

Two old Montagnards

There is one strange thing about this part of the world. Different peoples prefer to live at different altitudes. The Vietnamese are a people of the plains. To them "land" means ricefields. It is only recently that, finding the deltas over-crowded, some of the Vietnamese have begun to move into the uplands.

The Cambodians and Laotians also prefer low ground. The Thai people, however, are unhappy at heights of less than 3,000 feet (915 metres), and two other tribes, the Meos and Man tribe, refuse to live at less than 4,000 feet (1,220 metres).

Land cultivation varies with altitude, and with the people

who live at different levels. The Vietnamese, Cambodians and Laotians mostly grow rice. The others also grow rice, by the "dry" method of farming, but they also grow maize and other grains.

The Montagnards are *not* savages, but they are primitive. They may be descended from the original inhabitants of Vietnam who were driven into the mountains by the country's invaders.

They live in mountain country also inhabited by wild animals including tigers, elephants and goya—a wild buffalo which can kill a tiger in single combat.

Shrubs, thorns and elephant grass rise to a great height in this area which is not unlike the jungle of Burma. Occasionally the green and brown colours are brightened by a flame tree, with an enormous spread of brilliant crimson blossom.

The Montagnard houses are raised on wooden piles, as a protection against wild animals. The huts are long, many housing four or five families each. The people are quite friendly, and the headman of the village might want to make you his "brother" or his "sister".

For the ceremony you would climb up to the door of the hut, using a notched post. The hut has a timber frame, with woven leaf walls and thatched roof. The only things inside are large pots and palm leaf mats.

About one-third of the hut is a common room, used by all the families. Here they would gather to greet you. Their

A typical village in the highlands of Vietnam

fashions vary. Usually the men cover up the top half of the body, while the women wear rough wrapped skirts and nothing else.

Then you are invited to suck at a bamboo reed, the other end of which is stuck into a large pot filled with rice alcohol. You must not drink too much of it, for it is very potent and has a vile taste.

You hand over your reed to the senior women present— they are the real chiefs of the tribe; the mothers have great power, and tribal rights are passed on by the woman's side of the family.

26

A Montagnard mother and her child

Mountain tribeswomen drinking wine through hollow bamboo reeds

The people have their own forms of justice. If a man kills another—whether by accident or design—his crime can be made good by gifts to the gods and by a gift in cash or cattle to the dead man's family. Not even a murderer is condemned to death, for his ghost would haunt the village. A gift to the gods usually means a tribal feast.

More serious than murder is the theft of water or rice, both of which are under the special protection of the spirits. The punishment for this crime is banishment from the tribe.

The Montagnards have lived in their mountain jungles for centuries. Fear of the spirits governed their lives, and for long years their religion was based on winning the favour of local gods. However, under French rule they did make contact with the modern world. A difficulty arose about the languages they speak—they have very few words. One missionary explained

28

his difficulty: "When I was translating the New Testament into one of the Moï tongues," he said, "I came to the text, *God is love*. But there is *no* exact translation. The nearest I could get to it in this primitive language was: *The Great Spirit is not angry*. There is a slight difference!"

The French began to educate the people in what they called "penetration schools". From each village they collected boys of outstanding intelligence, gave them a good education—in French, and then sent them back to their villages to teach their people. Knowing only a Montagnard language, they would be condemned to elementary learning, but with French they could gain the knowledge of the world.

The French also taught them something new—work! The men of the tribes had previously only raised a few meagre crops, and hunted or fished a little. But when the French began to make roads in the mountains they had to have labour. The Montagnards needed a good deal of persuasion to work, but at last they did begin.

They are a brave people. They face the tiger armed only with spears or primitive cross-bows. They trap elephants and train them to work. The French thought that the Montagnards were too primitive to be soldiers, but the Americans have since proved that this was wrong.

The Religions of Vietnam

Although Vietnam is now a communist country, many Vietnamese are still members of religious organisations, and the government usually allows them to practise the religion of their choice.

Many follow the Chinese religion Taoism, and there are also very many Buddhists. In fact, it is possible for a person to be a Buddhist and a Taoist at the same time. Well over half the Vietnamese population are one or the other, if not both. These religions are, of course, very different from those of the primitive Montagnards.

Buddhism, in its early days, divided into two sects. One, called the Little Vehicle, believed what the Buddha himself taught—he was a teacher, not a god. This is the chief religion in Sri Lanka, Burma, Laos and Cambodia. In India, China and Japan, however, the Buddha is worshipped as a god, and many

A colourful pagoda. Vietnam has a rich tradition of ornamented architecture with a strong Chinese flavour

minor gods are worshipped with him. This religion adopted many ideas from the Hindu religion and, in China, it was affected by the teachings of Confucius and Lao-Tse. By the time it reached Vietnam, Buddhism was filled with ideas taken from many religions, with the Buddha as the chief god, but including ancestor worship and animism—the worship of gods and spirits supposed to live in trees, rivers or animals. A pagoda may display as few as a dozen or as many as a hundred gods.

Most families have a shrine in a corner of their house, with
an array of gods. One may be different from the others.

"Oh, that was our uncle," the householder may say.
"When he died, he left us a field and four cows; he was a very
good man. So we made him a god."

Such gods have of course very few worshippers. But one or
two new religions have been very successful.

Cao Dai, for example, claims more than two million members. It has accepted ideas from the best teachings of older faiths.
On its altars stand effigies of founders of religions like the
Buddha, Mahomet, Confucius, Lao-Tse—and Jesus Christ.
Among its "saints" is the great French author Victor Hugo. He
is believed to send messages to the present leaders, via the
spirits. The people take these messages very seriously.

32

Cao Dai not only has its own churches, but a cathedral as well. Its decorations are so colourful that you would suspect that Walt Disney was the architect. The religion has its own pope, archbishops and so forth. Women rank equally with men. A woman pope has not yet appeared, but there are women who are archbishops and at least one woman cardinal.

At one time Cao Dai was a real local power; like a state within a state. It owned huge areas of land around its capital, Tay Ninh. It collected its own taxes, and had its own private army. Its members are vegetarians and spiritualists. And, as in so many other religions, they have quarrelled a great deal among themselves.

A view of the Cao Dai temple in Tay Ninh

Buddhist monks with their traditional begging-bowls

Another new religion is Hoa-Hao, with a real belief in the supernatural. It also had local political power. At one time it made war on Cao Dai!

A third sect which mixed politics and religion was Binh Xuyen. Its founders were Chinese river pirates! It grew very wealthy and spent large sums on bribery.

Such bodies were a nuisance to their fellow-citizens and to their government, especially in the south during troubles

34

which followed the division of 1954. So the government of the time found itself having to deal with the private armies of religious sects as well as with those of political rebels.

This it did; but still some Buddhist priests had political influence, and they defied any government which annoyed them. They also opposed the Roman Catholic Christians who numbered fifteen per cent of the population; their ancestors had been converted to Catholicism during the period of French rule, and most remained firmly attached to their faith even after the French had withdrawn.

It can be safely said that the religious mix-up in Vietnam did much to weaken the southern half of the country, and to destroy its hope of becoming an independent democratic state.

The Temple of Remembrance in Saigon (now Ho Chi Minh City)

Life in the Towns

The Montagnards are the most primitive people in Vietnam. The most civilised people are to be found in the cities—particularly in Hanoi (the capital), and in Ho Chi Minh City which used to be named Saigon.

In Ho Chi Minh City, the main street leads direct from the docks to the cathedral. This seems reasonable. Trade and religion first interested the French in Vietnam.

Even though French rule ended in 1954, the centre of the city is still very French. True, the shops are of different kinds. The Chinese and Indians, the merchants of Asia, are well represented. Here is a woman's dress shop which might have been in Paris. On one side may be an Indian grocer; on the other a Chinese bazaar selling anything from jewellery to fish.

In the streets the people are, of course, mainly Vietnamese. Most of the men wear European dress—usually just trousers and a shirt because of the heat; but coolies (labourers) wear little more than a loin cloth.

Working women wear a little white jacket with black trousers. When they want to look their best, however, the women—and especially the girls—favour the *ao dai*—a sheath-like dress with a tight-fitting bodice, and a skirt split up each side, falling loosely over white satin trousers. You would think that Vietnamese girls had been sewn into their costume. And very pretty they can look in it.

These people look Chinese, but their complexions are light

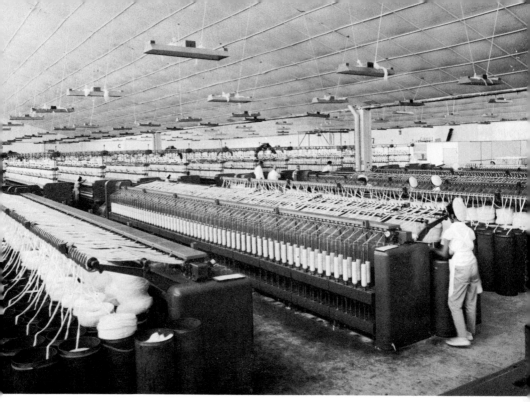

The girls in this textile factory all wear European-style clothes and and the plant they help to operate is absolutely up-to-date

brown rather than yellow. Their pleasant faces are matched by gentle voices—but if they get excited, the sound resembles the twittering of birds.

Down the main street pass cars, trucks and especially *cyclo-pousses*, sometimes called trishaws, or pedicabs. Once, not so many years ago, there were rickshaws, in the Chinese style, with a man running and pulling his passenger along. Now the passenger sits in a kind of bath-chair, behind which

is fixed a tricycle, on which a rugged coolie pedals away. He has probably hired the trishaw from a Chinese owner. It makes his living by day, and he sleeps in it at night.

There are some good buildings in the main streets of Ho Chi Minh city, and fine houses in the suburbs. Once these were owned by Frenchmen, or possibly by rich Chinese. But the side streets off the city centre are full of an interesting kind of Eastern life. Some people sleep on the pavement. Many do their work there. Here is a dentist, with a pile of extracted teeth as evidence of his skill. A barber props up a mirror against somebody's window and shaves his client. Men and women wash under a public water tap.

A girl wearing the traditional Vietnamese *ao dai*

Some of Vietnam's traffic jams include tri-shaws like this one, seen in a crowded street in Ho Chi Minh City

The Oriental does not love privacy or understand it. The pavement is his club.

There are many little stalls, offering highly coloured things to eat. Typical Vietnamese dishes include *Cha Gio* which is like a Chinese egg-roll, with a crust of rice flour containing shrimp, crab, egg, noodles, mushrooms and vegetables, finely chopped. Another favourite is *Bo Bay Mon*, meaning beef in seven dishes; and is just what it says—beef cooked in seven different ways. By contrast, *Chao Tom* makes a delicious sweet, with shrimp wrapped round sugar cane.

Merchants with trays wander up and down, offering the

most remarkable things for sale. Squatting on boxes will be shoe-shines, fortune-tellers and doctors. I never saw so many devices by which a man could earn a little by doing something for somebody else. There are even service stations where the men who pedal the trishaws can have their tyres inflated.

Few Eastern people wrap their food in paper. The Vietnamese are no exception. Here is a woman who has bought a fish: she has strung a piece of raffia through its gills, and carries it by the string. Here is a couple carrying a piece of pig's ear, also with string. And here is a man striving to fit a string loop round a piece of ice!

On the pavements there are red stains. The betel leaf is supposed to be good for the teeth, and people use it like chewing-gum, spitting out its juice: hence the red stains.

The markets are social as well as business centres. One, on a boulevard pavement, is called the Bird Market; all sorts of animals are sold there, from parrots to monkeys and squirrels to dogs. The Flower Market stretches along another boulevard, and is very colourful. Incidentally, the Botanical Gardens have one of the finest collections of tropical plants in the world.

The markets or shops sell all kinds of Vietnamese specialities. There are pictures painted in lacquer, requiring endless patience as layer after layer is added. There are carved statuettes in ivory or wood, and small objects made of tortoise-shell or crushed egg-shell.

40

Above all, the markets are fascinating for their people: those doing the shopping and the merchants who sell.

The Chinese and Indians are the natural tradesmen of the East. There are only a few thousand Indians in Vietnam, but there are well over a million Chinese. These form a very important part of the population.

Over three hundred years ago boat-loads of some three thousand Chinese arrived in what we now know as Ho Chi Minh City, and demanded land. The local ruler agreed, and gave them an estate at nearby Cholon.

The Chinese settled permanently. They prospered, and sent for their friends and relations. Their town grew; it was entirely Chinese, and it became rich. The Chinese have a gift for commerce; in the French days they controlled far more trade than did the French and the Vietnamese put together.

Ho Chi Minh City and Cholon now touch one another, but to pass from one to the other is like going into a different country. In Ho Chi Minh City the advertisements—there are quite a lot of them—are printed in Quoc-ngu, the written form of the Vietnamese language, using Roman letters—the sort we use. In Cholon everything is written in Chinese.

But the Chinese are not all alike—in their own country they have many varied languages and dialects. It is like this in Cholon, too.

The town has some sort of self-government. The people form five "congregations", or language groups, depending on the district of China from which their ancestors came. Their leaders collect taxes for the government, and arrange for schools, roads and welfare.

In the streets you might easily believe yourself to be in China; there are tall, over-crowded tenement houses, little cafés and even Chinese theatres.

You may even see an opium den in Cholon. Opium smoking has been unlawful in Vietnam for many years, but the Chinese in Cholon assured me that if you had enough money you could get your opium—or *anything* else.

The Vietnamese capital, Hanoi, is rather like Ho Chi Minh City but much smaller. It is a modern town—most of its

A typical display of locally grown fruit and vegetables in a market

ancient buildings were made of wood, and have long disappeared. By Eastern custom, the streets are often devoted to a single trade.

The French established a good university at Hanoi, a medical school, and many technical colleges, and they also used to send thousands of students to France. The university and the colleges are still there, but students who need overseas training are now sent to the U.S.S.R.

Apart from Hanoi and Ho Chi Minh City, only Haiphong has more than one million people. Very few other Vietnamese towns have populations of more than 100,000. However, some of the smaller towns are among the most interesting. For example, there is Hué, near the coast about half way between Ho Chi Minh City and Hanoi.

Hué was the imperial city of Vietnam. It was here that the emperors lived in the days of Vietnam's greatness. Like many capitals, it had fine buildings and monuments. Some of these have now disappeared, but enough remain to give an idea of the ancient glories of Hué.

The old city is quiet. It stands upon the River of Perfumes, dreamy and still. There are some ancient gateways and palaces, pagodas and royal tombs. These are actually outside the town. It was customary for an emperor to begin to build his tomb during his lifetime, so all are different and some of them very striking. Not all of them have escaped damage in twentieth-century fighting.

Hué was also a famous seat of learning. It became a centre

of patriotic feeling. An old city, it had some famous pagodas, whose monks preached not only religion but politics.

The little city has remains of old fortifications. There used to be two towns side by side—one Annamese and one French; the latter is now occupied by government officials and Chinese and other merchants. Outside Hué among the royal tombs, is one which displays the dead man's playthings and weapons— as well as a bed on which his spirit can rest whenever it revisits the tomb.

Today Hué is a rather down-at-heel place, but it used to be rich and powerful. When the Chinese captured it from the

Chams in A.D. 446, their booty was enormous. Among other things, they carried off a vast amount of pure gold!

South of the old capital, among the mountain forests, is the town of Da Lat. Its population used to be 50,000, but this was increased five times by refugees from the fighting after 1954. In happier times it used to be a very pleasant mountain resort, with cool air, and lovely walks around it. Tigers and elephants are not likely to come close enough to the town to cause trouble, but there are plenty of them in the nearby jungle-forests.

Not far from Da Lat is Ban Methuot, which used to be the emperor's country home. It is a small mansion, in mountainous country of forest and jungle.

This was the home of the last Emperor of Vietnam, Bao

The Pangour
waterfall near
Da Lat

Dai. He had a very strange life. Under the French he was ruler of Annam; then, during the Second World War, the Japanese occupiers of Vietnam made him a puppet emperor; for a time he was even political adviser to Ho Chi Minh, and afterwards the French made him emperor again—but with very little power.

He was a first-class shot—he bagged about twenty tigers in a year; any village suffering from raids on their domestic animals promptly appealed to the emperor. But, apart from this, he was not too well known in his own country, for he was a shy man who hated display, and had cut down expenditure on ceremonies. He married a charming lady who was not royal. Her name was Nam Phuong—"Fragrant Breeze of the South". His own family name was Vinh Thuy, and it was only when he became emperor that he adopted the name Bao Dai—"Guardian of Greatness".

When the French left Vietnam, Bao Dai retired with them, and settled in France.

The bicycle is the most popular form of transport throughout Vietnam. This particular street is in Hanoi

The Red River Delta

The Red River is really red—a dull brown-red—as it carries a great quantity of silt washed from northern valleys towards the sea.

The delta, which measures about 120 miles (193 kilometres) by seventy (113 kilometres), is over-populated. Though small, it is the home of about eleven million people. The soil is very fertile and, if the rains come regularly, two crops of rice can be grown each year. But even this is not enough; more rice supplies have to be imported.

The local houses are simple; they have mud walls and thatched roofs. The peasants of this region are small farmers, tilling their own land. Many villages have a market, where peasant women squat beside the eggs and vegetables they offer for sale. The rice-growing is hard work. The fields are enclosed not by hedges, but by low banks of dried mud. The field is flooded during the rains and, when it is swamped, the farmer brings his buffalo and ploughs the field; by now, the soil has become mud.

When the rains come the buffalo has to pull a plough through heavy mud. But in the dry season he is on holiday. Then he makes for the nearest stream and stands up to his nose in mud and water. He loves mud.

He is said to dislike women, but the local people deny this. But he *does* dislike Europeans. At least, he dislikes their smell. The buffalo has a very keen sense of smell and does not like the smell of the soap which Europeans use. Since the Vietnamese like to use lots of water but very little soap when they wash, the buffalo is less sensitive to their smell.

Ploughing ricefields

A buffalo resting

When the rainy season comes all the family get busy planting the rice seedlings one by one—a back-breaking job. Then there is a halt while the plants grow. As with most farming districts, the quality and quantity of the crop depend on the weather.

If a peasant does not own a buffalo he may borrow or hire one. In many villages, however, people are very neighbourly. In some, the buffaloes and other animals have always been owned by the whole village; the village Council of Notables decided who should use them. (These customs have prevailed for centuries, long before Vietnam became a communist country. Now the State controls everything—though it does make use of local organisations.)

The Council of Notables acts roughly like a European

All members of the
family have to work to
ensure their survival.
This picture shows
a peasant woman
winnowing in the
traditional Vietnamese
way

parish council. It decides who shall use the buffalo; if a road needs repairing, it sends men to do the work—peasants seldom have much money, and would rather do their share of local work than pay taxes.

There was an old saying often quoted in Vietnam: "The law of the king gives place to the custom of the village." The local headman is a very important person—the link between his village and the government.

There has never been enough land to go round in Vietnam, and most peasants in the delta region farmed so little that they barely made a living. Any man with a small piece of land was looked upon as rich. Some still have very tiny plots: they may add to their small income by fishing, or by working

50

for someone else in their spare time. Originally, they owned their little farms—they did not rent them from a landlord.

The peasant has always lived very simply. Usually he has two meals a day—breakfast, and a bigger meal at about 4 p.m. Rice is the most important food for all Vietnamese, wherever they may live.

If the family can afford it, fish and meat are a part of most meals. The fish may be fresh, but more often it is dried and salted. Perhaps next in importance after rice is a strong-smelling sauce called *nuoc man*. This is made by pressing layers of fish and salt together. An oil drops through from the tightly pressed layers of fish and salt. As the mixture is allowed to stand, sometimes outdoors in the hot sun, for weeks or even months, the smell of *nuoc man* oil is very, very strong! The sauce is eaten with rice, meat, chicken, fresh fish or vegetables.

A highland fisherman in his dugout boat

About fifty to sixty per cent of the Vietnamese diet consists of rice. About fifteen per cent is fish, fresh or salted, or poultry and other meat; the remainder, perhaps thirty per cent of an average family's diet, consists of vegetables. The Vietnamese like Chinese cabbage, potatoes, peas and beans. And most people like lots of seasoning, including garlic. Like the Chinese, the Vietnamese consider pork the finest meat.

With rice, fish, fish sauce and some meat, there is often a vegetable soup called *pho*. Among popular dishes are: lean pork, cooked with spices and called *cha-lua*; and slices of raw beef over which boiling water is poured, after which the beef slices are eaten with soya bean sauce.

Several pictures in this book show us that Vietnam is tropical. There are many palm trees. And, as in most tropical countries, there are fruits. There are bananas and oranges and, in the upland plateaux around Da Lat, wonderful strawberries and a few of the fruits that we find in our temperate climate. Fortunately, most people in Vietnam are able to buy fruit. There are also plenty of coconut palms, and the children sometimes enjoy a drink of cooled coconut milk.

On a market day, the peasants carry their produce to the nearest town. To do this they use the *don ganh*, or carrying pole, made from a length of split bamboo stem. It will carry considerable weights at each end, and bends only very little as the bearer jog-trots along.

He may carry baskets of rice, or a couple of pigs, each

A palm grove typical of many
of the tropical areas

trussed up into a bundle, and with its mouth tied so that it cannot even squeal.

Bamboo is the most useful plant of the north, as palm is of the south. The stouter poles support the house, while the leaves can be plaited into walls—as well as into mats or baskets. Slivers are used for wicker work, and finer slivers as string. Much of the furniture is made of bamboo. Peasant houses also contain metal and earthenware cooking pots, and a bed, or a jute hammock.

There is one other local plant which is put to good use. Sweets are terribly expensive, and pocket money is scarce. For a penny or two, however, a Vietnamese child can buy a piece of sugar cane to suck!

The Bay of the Dragon and the Big Hole

In the old days, if a man drawing a map knew nothing about the interior of a country, he would write: "Here be dragons." There are plenty of Vietnamese who still believe in dragons.

The Bay of the Dragon

Near the extreme northerly end of Vietnam is the Bay of Along—the Bay of the Dragon. It is beautiful and fantastic. If it were nearer to Europe or the United States of America, it would have millions of visitors each year.

The calm waters of the bay are usually dotted with the sampans—small boats—of fishermen, with their brown sails ribbed like bats' wings. All over the bay are islands—hundreds, thousands of them. Some are tiny rocks rising steeply from the sea; others are quite high and are covered with trees. Nearly all of them are covered in greenery. Some are honeycombed with caves. Some are separated from others by narrow channels. It is a lovely, amazing sight.

At sunset it is even more beautiful: the red rays tint the water and the bases of the islands disappear in the gloom, with only the tips of their rocks visible, a blushing pink. Then, by starlight, beauty of yet another kind appears. The bay is one of the most beautiful natural wonders of the world.

To the north of the bay is the biggest coal-hole in the world, at Cam Pha. It is not a mine—the top of a mountain has been sliced off, so that now the coal is close to the surface.

Never was coal-getting so simple. You run a truck along one of the terraces cut along the side of the mountain, and load it with coal. It is as simple as that.

When the coal was first discovered, the miners were asked to bore tunnels into the seam. They objected, fearing that they might disturb the earth dragons! Today they know

Cutting coal at Cam Pha

better, and they are interested not in dragons but in football.

Some of the miners are Chinese, and there used to be many more. By working at Cam Pha for a couple of years, they could save enough money to go home and buy a small farm. However, China and Vietnam have been on unfriendly terms in recent years, and so Chinese people are not as welcome as they were when the French ruled Vietnam.

The Mekong Delta

The River Mekong is long and mighty. It rises in Tibet, and flows through China into Laos. Then it forms the boundary between Laos and Vietnam, where it branches into a delta, reaching the sea in several channels, some of them very wide. From source to mouth it measures 2,800 miles (4,500 kilometres).

From June to October the rains caused by the monsoons lead to much flooding. From October to May the river occupies only a portion of its bed. The delta it forms is continually getting bigger as the river deposits on it the vast quantity of silt it carries down from the hills.

The land thus formed is very fertile. Hitherto there has been one difference between the peasants of the Red River delta and those of the Mekong: the former have owned their little farms, while the latter rented them from landlords. Often "share-cropping" was practised: in other words, the landlord was paid his rent not in money but in part of the crops.

It was not a good system, especially for the peasants. The landlord took from forty to fifty per cent of the crop. Since the expenses ate up something like another forty per cent, the peasant was left with only about ten per cent of what he had grown. But even in the French days this system was dying, and the landlord's share was reduced to twenty per cent.

Ricefields yield a rich crop, but the farmer has to work on them for no more than four months in a year. True, he may have some palm trees which yield up to twelve crops of coconuts a year, but they need little attention. Efforts have also been made to persuade the peasants to devote more of their land to growing vegetables. Another scheme introduced under French rule was that of teaching artisan crafts to the peasant, so that he could occupy himself during slack periods.

At least he has an assured market for his rice. Rice to the Asian is as important as bread to the European. And there have been some changes in recent years. Modern farmers in Vietnam use plenty of fertilizer. The use of fertilizers has increased rice production by forty or even fifty per cent. Although the Vietnamese farmer works his fields and lives much as did his ancestors, he has become a better and more scientific farmer. While the rice is growing, he uses

58

A farmer of the Mekong delta at work with his buffalo

insecticides to kill the grasshoppers, insects and beetles that might destroy the crop.

In addition to rice paddies, the lowland farmer always has a small vegetable garden. He raises a few chickens, ducks and pigs. These should supply the family needs for food. And if the farmer has a good crop, he has enough left over to sell in the town and city markets. As there are rivers and canals in many areas, as well as the sea coasts, there are always fish for sale.

Very few tractors are used in rice farming. This is partly because few people can afford to buy farm machinery. But another reason is that rice paddies are small, separated from other paddies by narrow dykes. Since the French left Vietnam, many of the big rice estates have been broken up and are now owned by farmers who once were sharecroppers. The average Vietnamese farm is very small. Not many farmers with so little land to cultivate, can afford machinery. Ordinary tractors would get stuck in the mud, but the Japanese have invented a machine for rice cultivation, and its use will doubtless spread.

Planting rice seedlings

The lowland farmer often keeps ducks

The villages in the Mekong delta region are usually built of timber from palm trees. Many houses are built on the brink of the river; some are on wooden piles overhanging it. No wonder that the children can swim almost as soon as they can walk.

When the French came to Indochina, they found very poor medical services on the Chinese model—a mixture of real knowledge and witch-doctoring. French doctors accompanied the army, and some of them stayed on. Now smallpox and cholera have been brought under control. The increase in population shows how successful the French health services were—sixteen million people in 1901, twenty-eight million people fifty years later.

The French trained some local men as doctors, and others as male nurses. The latter worked in villages, some running small medical posts. These trained medical orderlies could recognise and prescribe for common ailments, and would get more serious cases to hospitals in the nearest town.

After the French left, there came American aid. The Americans built and staffed many new hospitals. They also supplied village pumps, to supply plenty of good water.

The French missionaries were once active in the Mekong. Almost every other village seems to have a Catholic church—with a Vietnamese priest! Yet there is still much superstition in this region.

The Vietnamese are anxious for education. Like all peasant peoples, they have wonderful memories. Until the schools

Two Vietnamese nurses – they and their fellow-countrymen have now replaced the French doctors and nurses

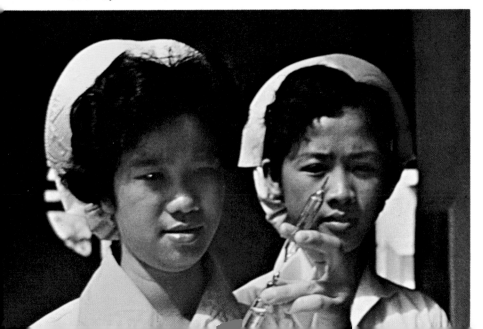

A village church. Like all the other buildings in the village, this Catholic church has a thatched roof

came, they gained all their knowledge by listening to others. Their knowledge and culture had been passed on verbally from one generation to another. Now the children are taught reading, writing, arithmetic and geography, and often other subjects as well.

Until the rainy season, the fields are brown. The delta is a huge plain, its flatness relieved only by groves of palm trees. Road traffic in normal times is heavy, if only because of the crowded population. The railways have four classes—the fourth class has a few wooden benches and plenty of standing or squatting room. It is always crowded, for it is cheap.

In the small towns there are trishaws or pedicabs; or jeeps with a chassis which is supposed to carry six passengers and usually carries ten. The jeeps are old, and because of this and the overcrowding, breakdowns are frequent.

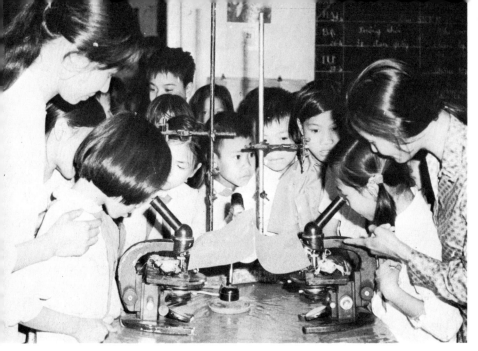
Children at Trung Vuong primary school in Hanoi

You might think that the buses employ sardine packers to get their passengers inside and their parcels on the roof. Trucks, too, are over-loaded; they are packed with merchandise, but there always seems to be room for a few people on top. I saw one truck carrying sixty pigs, in two layers— and a dozen passengers scrambled in on top of them.

Though life has been far from pleasant for them for many years, the Vietnamese are a cheerful people. To visit Vietnam at the time of one of its festivals is a wonderful experience. Some Vietnamese celebrate Christmas, but *all* celebrate *Tet*, the lunar New Year, which usually falls in Spring, and lasts for several days. The shops are joined by little booths, gaily decorated and lighted with fancy lanterns: here are sold fruit, toys and other presents.

Houses are decorated; there are family feasts; fire-crackers everywhere; music and smiles. Even the recent fighting often stopped for Tet!

Another national holiday is the Trung Sisters' day, in March or April. Two girls, representing the Sisters, and gaily dressed in costumes of the Trung period, ride elephants through the streets of the cities. They are escorted by guards in brilliant uniforms, and gaily dressed girls on horseback.

The Children's Festival is in the autumn, usually September or October. (All dates are based on the waxing and waning of the moon.) Tradition has it that the Emperor Duong Minh Hoang dreamed that he was in the land of the fairies where all was happy with merry-making and dancing.

Fruit stalls erected for Tet, the lunar New Year

A religious celebration in the streets of Saigon, now Ho Chi Minh City

When he awoke, he decided to organise such festivities all over the country. Gradually this became the Children's Festival, with gifts, special cakes, and dragon dances.

But now we must go back to the story we left uncompleted on page 14. Will you glance back at that, and then read on?

The Geneva Conference

At one time, Ho Chi Minh was considered merely as a nationalist patriot fighting against imperialists who wanted to rule his country. This was what some Americans believed—but they soon saw their mistake. By that time, it was too late for them to give any real aid to the French, but aid to Vietnam was another matter, and this was generously given.

On April 26th, 1954, representatives of France, the U.S.S.R. Britain and the U.S.A. met in conference at Geneva, anxious to find some way of ending the Vietminh war—to call it off as a draw, so to speak, as had happened in Korea.

The battle of Dien Bien Phu was then at its height, with the French and Vietnamese troops holding out bravely. On May 8th a French force made a last desperate bayonet charge. It failed, and the battle was over.

Naturally, the defeat of France affected the Geneva conference. But the results of the conference were reasonable. Prisoners of war were to be exchanged; Communist forces in Laos and Cambodia were to withdraw; France would retire from Indochina—but would still be active in commerce. Above all, Vietnam was to be divided. The area north of the 17th parallel of latitude was to belong to the Communists; and the south of Vietnam was to be a democratic state.

Refugees might leave either half for the other whenever they wanted. And elections were to be held in 1956.

The Communists were satisfied. They believed that now it was only a matter of time before they would control the whole of Vietnam. But a sudden difficulty arose. The United States refused to sign the Geneva agreement; so did Ngo Dinh Diem, the President of South Vietnam.

Soon, too, it became clear that the Communists did not intend to keep to the agreement either. Very many people wanted to leave North Vietnam for the South. About 900,000 actually did so, but Ho Chi Minh stopped another two million who wanted to go. He did not want to take over a country with hardly any inhabitants.

Diem was able, courageous and determined, and he had the advantage of generous American aid. The refugees from the North were an urgent problem. So were some of the sects who were political rather than religious, and who chose this disturbed moment to revolt against the government. Diem dealt with them firmly. He dismissed the Emperor Bao Dai, and he himself began to rule as a dictator. So great was the confusion in South Vietnam that this would have been accepted for the time being but for one fact—Diem was a Catholic.

In a true democracy this would not have mattered. But in a divided state like South Vietnam, where many factions had long striven to get power, and where the Buddhist priests were also politicians, trouble was certain. The Buddhists complained that Diem favoured the Catholics, and especially his own family.

Unity and discipline have never yet been known in Vietnam. First, some of the army units revolted. Then the Buddhist priests began to organise an opposition.

The Americans were alarmed. They had hoped that Diem would be not a party leader but a national leader. He was certainly competent. He dealt firmly with the refugee problem—and with the redistribution of agricultural land. A peasant share-cropper no longer had to pay more than twenty per cent of his crop to a landlord. Diem began to restore communications—by the end of the war not a bridge

Vietnamese mothers and babies at a clinic. Medical supplies often come from abroad

had been left standing. He made plans to enable farmers to buy machinery, and he did much to encourage education. In the meantime, the Americans were pouring food into the country, providing medical services, and helping to repair the war damage.

When the refugees from the North moved South, 100,000 of the Vietminh (Communist troops) from the South also moved North. Many others decided (or were ordered) to stay where they were, but they greased their weapons and buried them.

Ho Chi Minh knew the value of patience, but some of his followers were restless. The promised elections were *not* held in 1956; neither the U.S.A. nor South Vietnam had agreed to them, and it was clear that the Communists in North Vietnam would declare the results to be in favour of their government. In the following year, some of the Communists in South Vietnam dug up their rifles and began a civil war.

By this time, American soldiers had been invited into South Vietnam—not to fight, but to train a local army—just as the Chinese had done for the Vietminh. The Americans were very successful. In a couple of years they had trained and equipped an army to defend the 17th parallel. But then they found that the new army had to face a foe not at the frontier but within its own country!

We have seen that the headman is the vital link between the government and the village—and eighty-five per cent of the Vietnamese people live in villages. Now the guerrillas

American troops on patrol in South Vietnam during the war

began to murder the village headmen—more than six hundred of them in a year. The resultant confusion can be imagined. Some Vietminh who had gone as refugees to North Vietnam came back "home" to join their companions in fighting as guerrillas. They were armed and had been trained in guerrilla warfare. They forgot their old name, and became known as the Vietcong—short for Vietnam Cong San, or Vietnamese Communist Party. A new war had begun.

71

The Vietcong War

True, neither Diem nor the Americans at first realised this. The Americans were in South Vietnam only as instructors. Of course, they accompanied the units they trained when any action threatened, and could advise the Vietnamese officer, although he did not have to take their advice.

The new army guarded the 17th Parallel, which it had been trained to do. But the Vietcong recruits and reinforcements went round the boundary by crossing into Laos and using what came to be called the "Ho Chi Minh Trail".

For the Americans it was a new type of war; but it was familiar to the French. After a time, the Americans adopted ideas used by the British in their fight against the Chinese Communists in Malaya. Instead of trying to hold *every* village, they began to concentrate villages into "strategic hamlets", which were guarded. The people of South Vietnam were dismayed at the outbreak of a new war. Meanwhile, although Diem had to take stern measures to combat the Vietcong, his most dangerous enemies were closer at hand. The Buddhist leaders were determined to be rid of this Catholic.

Their method was peculiar. One day an elderly Buddhist monk squatted on a pavement in Saigon. Other monks poured petrol over the old man's robe, and he himself held a match to it. He was, of course, burned to death. This had been announced in advance, and all the pressmen were there.

The monk's protest aroused great indignation. Other people copied his example—even young girls burned themselves alive.

With their passion for freedom, the Americans had to support the Buddhist demand for it. They had long found Diem difficult, and now he deliberately rejected their advice. The principal centre of Buddhist activity in Saigon was the Xa Loi pagoda. Diem brought in Catholic units to attack it.

Buddhist monks outside a pagoda

Kicking and screaming monks and nuns were carried off in trucks—trucks supplied by the Americans for use against the Vietcong!

The Americans rebuked their ally. The army revolted, and Diem was killed. This did not bring peace to South Vietnam. It happened in 1963, and within a year the country had six new rulers. They were all generals, and each came to power by revolting against his predecessor.

The results were terrible. The country was in confusion because of the Vietcong war: if ever there was a time when unity was needed, it was now.

In Hanoi, President Ho Chi Minh sat biding his time, quite certain that South Vietnam would soon be under his rule. But then he made a great mistake.

Hitherto the Americans who had been killed had mostly been accompanying Vietnamese troops as advisers. This was a risk they had to face. But then, in February 1964, the Vietcong began to strike direct at the Americans—bombing their camps. This led to a different kind of war. At the time, the U.S.A. had only 16,000 men in South Vietnam—instructors and transport drivers. Now this force began to increase rapidly to a fighting army of 350,000 men.

At first, they had little more success than their allies. They had tanks and big guns, but the Vietcong were difficult to find.

The Americans would attack a military convoy and, by the time an avenging force arrived, the Vietcong would have disappeared—their soldiers would now be peasants working in their paddy fields.

The Vietcong information service was very efficient—they had agents in every village. Whenever they took a group of villages, they ruled the whole region around, levying taxes and seizing stocks of rice from the farmers. Nobody betrayed them: nobody dared to, for the Vietcong revenge was swift and terrible.

In the south, quarrels between Buddhists and Catholics were frequent. The Americans almost despaired of their thankless task. If they could have brought their enemies to battle, the war would have been won in an hour. But many American soldiers were shot without even seeing a Vietcong soldier.

The Vietcong had changed, too. The early Vietcong fighters were local men or returned emigrants from North Vietnam. Now, North Vietnam regular forces appeared on the southern battlefields. The war was "escalating", to use a popular word of the day—it was getting more fierce. The Americans struck back—from the air, where they held complete superiority. They carried the war into North Vietnam. True, their orders were to bomb definite military targets; pilots were only to attack communications. But now, there was a danger that the war might spread still further, and that China might join in.

While South Vietnam had been plunged into yet another war, what had been happening in the North?

The Communist North

Ho Chi Minh, like many another leader, was to find that victory was easy compared with the tasks which followed it.

A Communist country usually depends upon workers in the factories. But North Vietnam had not very many of these —the bulk of its people were peasant farmers, most of them owning the land they worked. So land was confiscated and landlords were either executed or sent to labour camps.

The confiscated land was distributed among other peasants—a "rich farmer" was defined as one who owned one small field! Then, the Communists began to form collective farms. The idea of these co-operative farms is good, but in practice they seldom succeed. A peasant is willing to work all hours tilling his own land, but is not so eager when working for someone else. The Vietnamese peasants were not encouraged by the fact that the collectives became State farms. Now they received a fixed wage instead of a share of the produce: the State became both landlord and employer rolled into one.

The confusion of these changes caused less rice to be grown, and supplies had to be brought from abroad. However, the government began experiments in the growing of maize, sugar, peanuts, tea, fruits and spices, and some of these were successful.

Also North Vietnam had most of the country's supply of coal, iron and other minerals, and most of the small factories. With help from China and the U.S.S.R., new factories were built. Some of these, too, were successful, some not.

Hanoi was a dull city, with little motor traffic; bicycles were

Harvesting the rice crop

the main method of transport. European newspapermen who visited Hanoi reported that the people were silent, and seemed sad. Once American planes began to bomb North Vietnam, life became more difficult, even though Hanoi itself was seldom bombed. Everyone had to get up at 5 a.m. and do exercises in the street before going to work, school or office. People worked until 9.30 a.m., then rested until 3 p.m. Work then continued until 9.30 at night. The reason for these unusual working hours was that people expected American planes to bomb the city during the middle of the day so as to kill as many people as possible.

There were pictures of "Uncle Ho", as he was called, everywhere. Life was drab. Most people wore a kind of grey-blue battledress. Loudspeakers in the streets blared out music and political talk. Unskilled factory workers earned a very low wage, and farm-workers earned even less. The Press was controlled by the government, and there were plenty of police to enforce the law. People were encouraged to give information about any friends and neighbours who might not agree with the government and its policies. Everybody was suspicious of everybody else.

Ho Chi Minh was popular nevertheless. The young people were enthusiastic about his government. So, too, were large numbers of friendly if misguided Americans and other foreigners. But the government's success depended on the standard of life which it gave to its people. This could scarcely be improved until the war ended.

78

Villages at War

In those war years Saigon, the capital of South Vietnam, suffered occasional bomb explosions and assassinations. But it was the villages which carried the full weight of the war.

For example, Kien Ninh was a village some distance from Saigon in the Mekong delta. It suffered in the war with the French. Then, when peace came and the Vietminh could move to the new Communist state in the North, the villagers were astonished to find that a dozen Vietminh had lived for years unsuspected in their midst.

There followed a few uneasy years of peace. American aid was very welcome: it gave a good water supply for the village, helped to rebuild the school and gave a medical service. The villagers went on growing rice.

Then the Vietcong war began. The village headman was murdered, and a successor was appointed. He, too, was killed. People were afraid. The terror had returned.

The government sent a few soldiers to advise on the village

A Vietnamese patrol during the war between North and South

defence. The wooden watch-tower, used in the French period, was repaired. A Home Guard force was recruited, its members were given old rifles, and ordered to defend their village.

For weeks nothing happened. Then came a Vietcong raid. The Home Guard could do little: the few men on watch were kept quiet by heavy fire while the raiders entered the village by another way.

The raiders were well informed. They included men who had previously fought for the Vietminh against the French. They knew which of the villagers were against them—and the houses of these people were burned down. So everybody realised that if you opposed the Vietcong, your house would be destroyed. It was better, they decided, to stand aside.

Another raid followed. The outnumbered Home Guard

fired a few shots and then surrendered. Then the men of the village were assembled. A Vietcong officer announced that they must make "voluntary contributions" of rice to the Vietcong—and he read out a list of the quantity each man should "give". The peasants were alarmed. But what could they do—the Vietcong men had the guns. Half the village stock of rice was carted off.

The new headman managed to get a message through to the nearest town. About noon next day government troops

A wooden watch-tower used for village defence

arrived—they were far too late: the Vietcong had disappeared.

The village defences were improved. A deep, wide trench was dug all round the village, and on its floor *pungees* were planted. (These are sharp, pointed bamboo stakes, which are so hard that they will pass through a man's shoes and cripple him.) The Home Guard defence force was doubled.

But there was great disquiet. Some of the villagers had recognised some of the men among the Vietcong. These were peasants from a neighbouring village! By the time the troops arrived, these men would be working as usual in their paddy fields. Who could suspect they had spent the night as soldiers!

Now it became known that most of the district was controlled by the Vietcong. One day two of them arrived, armed. They demanded that the village should pay its taxes to them. The headman protested: the taxes had already been paid to the government. This was no use. If the village did not pay the Vietcong, men would come and take it by force—doing much damage and maybe killing some of the people.

For a while there was a lull. Sounds of battle were often heard, and visitors brought news of the fate of villages which had defied the Vietcong. There was a great fear in Kien Ninh.

Everybody knew what must come, but no one knew when.

The watch-tower commanded the one road leading to the village. Traffic could move by day, but the night belonged to the Vietcong.

So they came by night. They ignored the watch-tower and

82

South Vietnamese villagers constructing palisades to protect their village from guerilla attacks

its pitiful little garrison, and approached by forest paths. And a local sympathiser was there to show them the way through the rows of pungees. When the local people got up the next morning, they found that their village was controlled by the Vietcong.

The invaders needed more rice. The headman vainly protested that there was scarcely enough left for the village use.

Evidently the Vietcong were going to stay—or most of them, anyway. These were long-service soldiers: the local men went back to their homes.

The others selected billets in the cottages, posted sentries, and lay down to rest. They were tired: two days earlier they had attacked another village in the delta area.

In Kien Ninh there was a boy of thirteen; he was the son of one of the murdered headmen. He had slipped out of the village during the early part of the attack, following paths through the forest to the riverside. There he found a fisherman's boat, and he went in it to the nearest town.

American as well as Vietnamese troops were there. The officers at once planned an attack on Kien Ninh. A small force could travel by water. Far more soldiers would move towards the village by truck, seeking to surround it. The task force included artillery: maybe a few shells would frighten out the Vietcong, who could then be shot down as they dashed for the shelter of the forest.

The operation was not without its dangers. A truck struck a Vietcong mine and blew up, killing a dozen soldiers. A man on a forest track had his foot blown off when he too trod on a mine.

The troops surrounded the village. The guns began to fire; some of the wooden houses were set alight. The people were rushing from the village—they were really running away in terror, but the soldiers thought they were Vietcong. Then an American officer saw women and children among them, and immediately ordered a cease fire.

Not one Vietcong soldier was found in the village. They had their spies not only about the countryside but in the military headquarters. One was a radio operator, and he

84

The Vietnamese climate means that many military operations involved crossing flooded areas like this one

slipped in among his official messages a warning to the Vietcong that an attack on Kien Ninh would begin.

That was not quite the end of the episode. A few nights later the Vietcong again raided the village. They kidnapped the boy who had warned the troops, and took him away. He has never been seen or heard of since.

Then there was quiet for a few weeks, and during this time the people's fear grew. So did their suspicion. Some of the villagers had been killed or wounded by the Americans—who were supposed to be their friends. Were they not just as bad as the Vietcong? What were these Americans doing here, anyway? Probably they had come to conquer Vietnam for themselves, the simple people thought—they did not realise that such ideas were being put into their heads by Vietcong agents. In their distress they forgot about the aid they had received from America. They were too frightened to think.

The New Republic

It had gradually become clear that neither the Vietcong nor the forces in South Vietnam were winning. The Vietcong could not defeat the Americans with guerilla warfare, and the Americans could not hope to defeat the Vietcong unless they cut off their sources of supply. This meant that they would have to invade North Vietnam, and if they did so the U.S.S.R. and China would certainly come to the aid of their fellow Communists. A third World War would surely follow, and no country wished to be responsible for that. So the Americans began to suggest talks about peace.

At first, and for several years, neither the Vietcong nor the government of North Vietnam showed any serious interest in such talks. They appeared to believe that if they held out long enough the Americans would give in more and more to their wishes—especially a North Vietnam take-over of South Vietnam.

In a sense, that is what finally happened. When peace talks were held at last, the Americans agreed to withdraw from Vietnam, and they began to move out during 1973. No doubt they hoped that the two Vietnams would now go their separate ways peacefully, as had been expected after the country was divided, back in 1954. In fact, the Vietcong, with support from North Vietnam, would not let South Vietnam live in peace.

This park in Hanoi was renamed Lenin Park in 1976 to celebrate the reunification of the two parts of Vietnam

Without American help, and with a weak and not very popular government, South Vietnam could no longer defend itself. By April 1975, it had been overrun, and at the end of that month its army surrendered. Vietnam was now one country again—but a communist country, controlled by the government in Hanoi.

Hanoi now set up a "puppet" government for the south, and in the following year held elections for the whole country. Many people thought that these elections were undemocratic, and even dishonest, but in any case there was very little choice for the voters. Every candidate had to be a supporter of Hanoi's communist constitution, and the elected candidates became a National Assembly (parliament) for a new nation called the Socialist Republic of Vietnam. The republic became a member of the United Nations Organisation in 1977, and of Comecon (the "common market" of some communist countries) in 1978. It has a red flag with a five-pointed yellow star in the centre, and a rather aggressive national anthem called *Tien Quan Ca*, which means "The troops are advancing".

As if to show that the national anthem meant exactly what it said, Vietnam was soon marching troops into neighbouring Cambodia (Kampuchea) to support a communist revolution there. It has kept troops in Cambodia ever since, as the revolutionary government appears to be unpopular, and could not survive without them. However, their presence keeps Vietnam on very good terms with the U.S.S.R., which also supports the new Cambodian government. Indeed, it seems likely that the invasion took place only because Vietnam had agreed to a 25-year treaty of co-operation with the U.S.S.R. on joining Comecon.

On the other hand, the attack on Cambodia brought another old friendship to an end. China did not approve of the new Cambodian government, or of the part that the U.S.S.R. and Vietnam had played in the revolution. It therefore invaded the north of Vietnam while Vietnam was invading Cambodia. This invasion did not last long. The Chinese troops moved out about a month after they had marched in, but the two countries have remained unfriendly to each other.

Meanwhile, in Vietnam itself the new government had come up against problems, and was finding that its policies were neither wholly popular nor wholly successful.

Vietnam's Future

Vietnam is only one of the many countries which, when freed from colonial rule, have found themselves involved in civil war and in wars with their neighbours. Very often such countries have also found themselves worse off economically than they were under colonial rule—less able to provide work, food and services for their people. Wars are partly to blame for that but by no means wholly to blame. Most of these countries can never hope to support themselves; they will always be dependent on outside help.

Vietnam is quite different. With continued peace, it could support its people on a decent standard of living—indeed, for Asia, a high standard of living. In normal times it can feed itself and export a considerable amount of rice. It produces large quantities of sugar, tea, coffee, livestock, fish, tobacco, rubber, cotton and timber. It has plenty of coal and other useful minerals and some well-established factories producing mainly

Vietnamese refugees made homeless by the long and fierce war

cloth, fertilizers and paper goods. However, the socialist republic has not been very successful in using or developing Vietnam's resources and has even had difficulty in providing enough food for some parts of the country.

To some extent, these troubles were caused by typhoons and floods which destroyed crops and livestock but they are also the result of government promises and plans which have not proved very popular either at home or abroad. Many farmers resent having to work for fairly low wages on large "co-operative" farms instead of tending their own small farms as they did formerly. Many businessmen resent having had their businesses taken over by the government, even when the

90

government allows them to remain as manager or advisor. And few foreign countries, except the U.S.S.R., are prepared to give aid to a country which is putting so much money and man-power into such ventures as the invasion of Cambodia.

One result of all this is that the republic has become more and more dependent upon the U.S.S.R. which has now taken over all the exploration for oil and a large number of building projects in Vietnam. Another result is that Vietnam has lost some of it most intelligent, efficient and highly-skilled people. Since 1976, one million or more have moved to Thailand and other Asian countries, as well as to more distant countries such as Britain, the U.S.A. and Australia. Many of these were so anxious to leave Vietnam that they travelled as "boat people"

A new irrigation system. In spite of the war, Vietnam is look-ing towards a more productive and pros-perous future

in small, over-crowded and dangerously old ships, with no certainty that they would reach a country willing to give them refuge. And it is clear that many more still want to leave.

In spite of these problems, there have been signs that life for most Vietnamese has been improving a little since 1981. The government has certainly been doing more to encourage interest and aid from countries other than the U.S.S.R. and also to ease some of the pressures on farmers and businessmen. Perhaps the republic's second five years may give the Vietnamese more opportunity to be the peaceful, happy people that they are by nature.

A young citizen of Vietnam. Let us hope that the country will find solutions to at least some of its many problems so that she is ensured a healthy and happy future

Index